Tough Luck

Tough Luck

Poems

Todd Boss

W. W. NORTON & COMPANY

Independent Publishers Since 1923

NEW YORK | LONDON

For information about permission to reproduce selections from this book,
write to Permissions, W. W. Norton & Company, Inc.,
500 Fifth Avenue, New York, NY 10110

For information about special discounts for bulk purchases, please contact
W. W. Norton Special Sales at specialsales@wwnorton.com or 800-233-4830

Manufacturing by LSC Communications Harrisonburg
Book design by JAM Design
Production manager: Louise Mattarelliano

Library of Congress Cataloging-in-Publication Data

Names: Boss, Todd.
Title: Tough luck : poems / Todd Boss.
Description: First edition. | New York : W. W. Norton & Company, [2017]
Identifiers: LCCN 2016058733 | ISBN 9780393608625 (hardcover)
Classification: LCC PS3602.O8375 A6 2017 | DDC 811/.6—dc23
LC record available at https://lccn.loc.gov/2016058733

W. W. Norton & Company, Inc.
500 Fifth Avenue, New York, N.Y. 10110
www.wwnorton.com

W. W. Norton & Company Ltd.
15 Carlisle Street, London W1D 3BS

1 2 3 4 5 6 7 8 9 0

For my daughter

Contents

An Approach to This Book

On August 1, 2007, in downtown Minneapolis, a major interstate bridge—jammed with six lanes of evening commuters—collapsed, mightily, in sections, into the broad urban canyon of the Mississippi River, killing thirteen people and injuring scores more.

I'd crossed the bridge twenty minutes before it fell.

The Minneapolis-St. Paul metro area went into a state of shock. The metro traffic system convulsed. The sound of every kind of siren screaming at once called us to our radios and televisions. News helicopters floated above the scene. The world was gawking. The bridge, in disjointed sections of twisted decking—littered with sedans, delivery trucks, a school bus—looked like an elaborate model set dropped by a reckless toddler.

Something terrible had been made abundantly apparent. Apparently there was danger in the everyday. Apparently the I-35W Bridge had been a time bomb, ticking in the summer heat. Apparently we'd been playing a kind of rolling roulette—all of us—loading the aging bridge hour after hour with freighted tons of loved ones.

And I do mean *all of us*. In 2013, the American Society of Civil Engineers issued a report that applied the words "structurally deficient" or "functionally obsolete" to no fewer than 66,749 of America's bridges—fully one-third of the total bridge decking in the country.

Back at home, my twenty-year marriage, too, was collapsing into ruin—an experience that, for me, was just as foundational. In the end, when our children were asking us to get a divorce, breaking the family seemed like the most constructive thing I could do. But it was agony. I pray I experience no proximal despair in this lifetime, nor any as prolonged.

I've since moved from that suburban bedlam to a tiny downtown loft where, if I walk just a block downhill, I can stand alongside the Mississippi River. The views here are tremendous. Upstream is Saint Anthony Falls, a blue-velvet 275-foot-wide spillway cascade that once powered the mills that gave birth to Minneapolis. Downstream is the new I-35W Bridge that was built in place of the fallen one. Its approaches and landfalls form neat clusters of clean concrete overpasses and ramps. Lit blue at night, its chilly indifference seems ill-mannered, given the collapse that preceded it. I wonder how long it'll hold up under the weight of its expanded eight lanes of vehicles.

Those on foot prefer the much older, statelier Stone Arch Bridge—a landmark on the National Register—which curves gracefully from amongst the tastefully converted mill district condos lining the downtown side of the river to the still cobbled main street of old Saint Anthony. When I cross this bridge, I can feel myself go as calm as the river's broad surface. The city's scale turns human. In the right breeze, I get the mist from the falls on my face.

I try to avoid clichés as a professional imperative, and the phrase "they don't make them like they used to" is one I avoid doubly, because it makes me sound old. And yet, you only need to run a hand over my great-granduncle's Steinway, for example, or the iron letterpress in my studio, or the wall-mounted grinder I crush my coffee with every morning, to feel how much craftsmanship and old-world integrity have gone, dare I say, under the bridge.

As hobby farmers, my parents trained me in the industrial and agricultural arts. They loved well-made things, and it grieved me that my marriage crumbled in their sight.

Maybe I love writing poetry because occasionally it delivers the satisfaction of having built something worthwhile with my hands. Or maybe I love the sturdy marriage between writer and reader—a marriage whose terms, patterns, and narratives are set down and won't deteriorate or get rewritten. Maybe I love the sense of tension-and-release—of suspension—one feels when one reads a poem, the rise and fall of the metaphorical view on either side, and the sense of arrival at the end.

I suppose I'm sensitive to such things. I've got my reasons.

But we're all crossing, aren't we, from one place to another.

So no doubt you've got yours.

Tough Luck

When My Mother Says *Tough Luck*

it's like the rough tongue of
leather in a boot somehow,

the way you dig your
thumb in there when it gets

stuck to curl it out again
against the topside

of your foot and pull it flat
so you can truss it up,

or like the slap of milk
on milk in a metal bucket

carried up the ramp
to be dumped in the bulk–

house tank with the rest,
or the clank of the bucket

handle against the bucket's
flank once the milk's

poured out and the bucket's
done its chore, or like the

prayer a shucked–off pair
of garden gloves cough

softly when they're chucked
from the hand and land

filthy on the back porch floor.

Accounting

Its fine
incisors
grinding

my mother
fed my
father's
fledgling
carpentry
concern
into her
adding
machine

as if its
hunger
could be
satisfied

costs &
savings
spooling
to our
wooden
kitchen
floor &
pooling

amounting
to nothing

a shop tool's
shavings.

Line-Dried Laundry

is by lifting and
    lifting in
        wind awhile en-

livened, sheets
    crispened, denim
        roughened,

kitchen cottons
    more apt to
        cotton to ab-

sorption as if
    from one
        hour in sun

they'd relearned
    thirst or some-
        thing. You

might be for-
    given if in
        your imagination

wind and light
    acquired a
        mythification

with or without
    your intention.
        You might be

forgiven for
    keeping
        between your

thumb and fore-
  finger for-
    ever some

fond
  recollection of
    wooden pins

in all their
  wind-worn
    nudity.

You might even
  run a hand
    over an idle

pump handle
  one day
    as if to say

I knew you when.

But look at me,
  talking to

farmers again.

When My Father Says *Toughen Up*

it's like the clop of the walnut
block beneath the gavel of the

judge who fits the punishment
to the crime, or like the pop of the

velveteen seedpod of the lupine
finally scattering its ordnance of

shot amongst the hollyhock,
or like the aftershock of a

Massey Ferguson engine cut off
too hot, that *chuff* out the muffler

that echoes off the pole barn
sharp as a whooping cough,

or like the upstart of a startled
ruffed grouse thumping into

flight right beside you on a walk,
or like the hard clap on the back

you get when you choke, as if
to congratulate you. He doesn't

say it to berate you, he says it to
hike you up an inch or two, like

when he took you by the collar
when you were little to zip you

into that boiled wool jacket he
sent you out to chores with,

or like the high salute we send
soldiers to wars with.

For an Old Runner

Last time I was out to the farm, I found
a sleigh runner made of timber, banded in iron,

rusting in the machine shop under the granary.
It was my father's father's father's father's,

and I know I had no business bringing it home
without asking Donny—my second cousin, who

owns and farms the land around the abandoned
farmstead now—but here it hangs, crosswise

on a wall in my study. Its blunted nose eighteen hands
high, it arcs above my head, and when I reach

to touch it—as for want of the feel of old wood I
will from time to time—I might as well be handling

one of the horses that hauled it, its neck a rough
relic, so rough it's almost smooth with roughness,

its whole body—in the wall beside me imaginary—
haunch-heavy but simultaneously holding

weightlessly still for me, eyes steady, ears keen,
and ready the way horses are always ready, even

stolen horses, even horses one has never driven,
never even seen.

When We Say *Knuckle Down*

we mean there's torque to be
doubled, the way the quarter-
horse recouples her shoe-heavy

hooves, head down, and throws
herself forward, we mean
the load in the sled demands a

hard haul ahead, the hill to be
taken as a problem not of moment
but momentum, we mean

the chili will taste better once
the bitter bread of winter's eaten,
slashing our faces sheet on sheet,

just as in summer we mean
it matters not how hot the sun
if there are chores to be done.

The knuckles have nothing
to do with it really, not the ones
around reins or handles, not

the ones we wring like rags over
figures evenings—no we don't
mean those—we mean the knuckles

of our wills, those folding bones
in there somewhere where our
lives have hold of the land—

we mean that the whole body,
the whole mind, the whole
damned soul is a goddamned hand.

Antiques

She hardly knew her grand- or great-grandparents, save a
    memory of
a day when, six years old, she sat beside a man as old as Time
and learned from him to shell dried field-corn off the ear,

mimicking by placing her small thumbs together just as his
great work-worn ones, thick-nailed and heavy-knuckled, were . . .

.   .   .

I've often wondered why it was antiques my mother gravitated
    toward.
She labored to restore them as if labor were its own reward.
She wasted nothing, ventured much, questioned what she
    couldn't touch,

and times were such and we were far afield enough
that there was still, on auction lists, a great variety of good old
wooden farmhouse stuff my mother could get cheap. She
    learned

to read between the lines of Thursday's auction ads and
    underlined
the very pieces that, on Sunday, she would reap from some
    white
stand-alone Victorian three counties off, surrounded by a barn

and cribs and gardens gone to rot. A death was always in the air,
the livestock gone, a window plugged, a haze of absence
    everywhere.
A country auction is a wake for property. It's mostly

neighbors, curious about the inner lives of those who've passed,
that come. But some are there for bargains: lumber, tractors,
wagons, anything useful goes. My mother's number rarely rose

from out her shirtfront pocket while brass beds and rusted
rakes and hoes and sleds were sold. It only fluttered forth for
      things
of solid oak or cherry that her elders might've had: a busted

loveseat once, a sturdy secretary built to last. Always she was
slow to start the bidding and to end it fast. The hallways
of the stranger's house—which yesterday in twos and threes

men lent their balances and gravities to bring this highboy,
that buffet, and set them gently in the front yard grass—
would empty out at last. And later those same men, hoisting it
      again

at count of three, would carry the one she'd won behind
my mom and me to where she'd parked my father's pickup truck
and lay it in, on rugs or tarps she'd brought, then wish her luck

and wave us off. It always had some chipped or faded slop
of paint in layers on it, which is why she'd got it for a sonnet.
That was the genius of her art. Just judging by its weight, or feel,

or looking underneath its glass, or pulling drawers, or other such
inspection she could tell what lay beneath its coats of primer,
      milk,
and gloss. She knew its heart. And sure enough, in later weeks,

our basement reeks of thinner, and by putty knife and wire scrape
the gunk shucks off in peels and muddy clots, and there at last
in perfect nudity it stands: its grains, its pearls, its knotty

curls, its rays and flecks of quarter-sawn or hand-turned parts
revealed. And now she's stirring Danish oil. And now she dips
a rag of cotton in. And now she rubs into its naked grain

three fingers' width of gold as blond as wheat. And now
the house smells pungent sweet. And soon we'll have a seat
or table in the living room that once was something no one

wanted much—made lovely by my mother's touch.
                                                    "And what if
this is all there is?" she asked me once when I had grown and
      made
mistakes, and she was tired, accepting of her lot in life. And yet

her life was filled with things she had, by loving them, restored.

                        .   .   .

The soul runs deep, but still will keep a color in the board.
Last year I asked her why it was antiques she'd always gravitated
      toward,

and—once she'd weighed the question for a while—rolled
it hand to hand like an old hand-mirror lost and found—she told
a half-memory of a six-year-old . . .

Grinding Pepper

        reminds us:
even
        shoulder
and wrist
        go to grist.
Every
        twist
acquaints us
        with the
crepitus
        within us.
You can feel
        each
piperine
        pip
splint and
        pulver as you
twist one
        cylinder over
the other and
        let the in–
consistent list of
        peppercornage
litter your
        meat or
whatever.
        Doesn't it
smell a
        bit like
danger.
        Doesn't it
gride
        like pride
grides

on the grind-
stones of ambition.
    Isn't there
precognition
  in the sound.
All's bound
  to be ground
to ash
   and dust,
a single mill
  millwheeling it.
Your last
   collapse
will feel
   like this
though
   you'll be
long past
  feeling it . . .

A Little Hard Work Won't Kill Ya

was their mantra
when I begrudged
the chores I got.

The gulag it's not,
my mother said.

Or she quoted that
fairy-tale cluck:
And who will help
me *eat* the bread?

My dad just shook
his head, said Tough
it out, said Tears
won't get it done.

Now they lament
my childhood went
like firewood:
cut, split, stacked
and gone.

Restraint

A three-point
harness it ain't.
Its threads are
thin, the kind
arachnids spin.
We think we
have it, but we
don't. We eat
and drink and
say and think
and repeat
what we say we
won't. We go
despite bright
gossamers of
no. It's on least
gusts of yes
we blow, with
no tomorrows
in our plans.
There are no
pylons between
spans. There are
no limits on
the dash. We
call it "accident,"
the crash.

All the Dropped

arguments
, all the cropped
thoughts

. They collect
. They amount

. Dead claims
, lost
causes and
hopes given up

—they gather
—they must

. A dust
, they cover
whatever we
own

. A rust
, they wear
our best
works down

. A
garden
of winter
seeds

. We drown
in undone
deeds

.

When You Say *You Suck*

you prick you jerk you
sick weak pathetic piece of

crap, you yank every rug,
you rock the house off

its block, you cock the
roof, you knock the cul-de-

sac for a loop, you make
big demolition booms ex-

plode through the kids'
rooms, blast the glass and

drapes from their casings,
unjamb the door, jump

the silver in the drawer,
shiver the stemware, surge

your electric rage through
the grid, fritz the lights,

trip the network, and dim
like the dimming west

the sequins in the dress
our daughter keeps pressed

in what we all still call her
hope chest.

Liquor Store

Every day new ways to ask it.
I could fill a shopping basket.

I could stock a liquor store
with *Does she love me anymore.*

Congratulations

I kept thinking there was a word
a grand-master-championship-level word
that used all seven of my tiles
and intersected the entire 15x15 square board
using letters from four or five other words
and racking up several double-word scores
and triple-letter scores besides
the cumulative total of which
could still win the game for me despite
the dizzying array of lexical fireworks
you'd been setting off all around me
for years but there never was
and I ended up playing words like
uh and um and oh and leaving
the rest of my letters sitting there in the tray
like dumbstruck parishioners
and counting them up to subtract them
and congratulating you quietly in the end.

My Double

has finally
walked. We
talked, but it
was no use,
he'd made
up his mind.

So, Baby—
do you want
me to find
another zero
who'll take
your abuse

(a good one
who'll pass
as your hero
might take
me months)

or are we
done now,
maybe,
with stunts?

Rocket

Despite that you
wrote your name
and number
on its fuselage
in magic marker

neither your quiet
hours at the kitchen
table assembling
it with glue

nor your choice of
paint and lacquer

nor your seemingly
equally perfect
choice of a seemingly
breezeless day
for the launch of
your ambition

nor the thrill
of its swift ignition

nor the heights
it streaks

nor the dancing
way you chase
beneath its

dot

across that
seemingly endless
childhood field

will ever be
restored to you

by the people
in the topmost
branches of whose trees

unseen

it may yet from
its plastic
chute
on thin
white
string

still swing.

They Mate for Life

Swans
don't laugh.

Geese
don't either.

No gander
ruffles
his spouse's
eider.

Sad–faced
gibbons
make as sober
a culture
as angelfish
or turkey
vulture.

They mate
for life
like the turtle
dove,
but none
would survive
a human love.

When I Said *I Quit*

it felt

like shit. I tasted
the filth

of fouled vows
in my spit.

I let sorrow
give way

like an opening
pit. I lost

weight, lost
work, lost

my sarcastic
wit. I went

crazy a little
bit. But

guess what?
They

were the
right words

and these
were

slight fees
and

just like
new keys

they fit.

Folds

A bleat

from the lost
and shivering flock

of migraine sleep
and you've asked

for the black sheep
we call Baa

who went with you
everywhere

till you were twelve
and so from

the croft in your
closet where

outgrown you
propped him

we fetch him, and
tuck him into

your arms too weak
to take him close

and how thin and
how sweet

are the peals that ring
from the mountainside

chapels we didn't
know were near

and that only
you can hear

as you fall back in
among the folds.

Bravery

A rung's
come broken in the
ladder to the mow

and so one hesitates
to clamber up there
just to bomb a cow
with dung or bother
swallows from their
rafter cakes. It takes
a new footing some-
where in the ribs'
treads, about heart-
height, to climb it
now. A new gap's in
the smile that smiles
from the limed barn
floor. There seems
to come a break in
the war. But then one
of the neighbors' sons,
too young to know it
was otherwise once,
braves it—and soon,
even with a sweater-
swaddled kitten or a
BB gun, all the kids
can do it again, nearly
at a run, like pros, and
so it goes, as before.

An Earthquake Leaves a Building

b rok e n in tact—
f rac tu red   thr ougho ut
w ith out   outw ar d
signs o f spide r-
webbing displa yed.
I n fact it 's   re made,
re- m orta red, ha vin g
b ee n h alved and
quar te red, ei gh thed
an d   16the d, 3 2nde d,
64 th e d, et cete ra,   in
p ro portio ns   in-
creas in gly in   exact.
So   a heart can be
cracked   and sti ll
fu nctio n after gr eat
co m mot ion , b eat
de sp ite th e beating it' s
taken, an d eve n s helter
t he s hak en perso n.

Fragments for the 35W Bridge

The
river
enters
the
gulf
and
the
gulf
enters
the
sea
et cetera
like
the
blood
of
gods . . .
every
water
the
same
water
coming
round . . .
every day
someone
staring
into
time
whispering
mistakenly:
only
here . . .
only
now . . .

2

My
cousin
called
from
across
town
the
hour
the
bridge
went
down.
Are
you
okay?
Fine,
fine,
I
said.
Good-bye,
Good-bye.
The
call
went
dead.
But
I
love
my
cousin.
So
I
held
the
line.

3

Minnesota's
fifth-
busiest,
freighting
140,000
vehicles
daily,
"Bridge
9340"
carried
eight
lanes
of
Interstate
Highway
35W
.3
miles
along
14
spans
115
feet
above
Mississippi
River
Mile
853
till
it
fell,
injuring
145,
killing
thirteen.

4

And
where
had
they
been
going,
those
thirteen
gone?
—Dinner
with
a
friend.
—Bakery
customers
all
over
town.
—Greek
folk
dancing
lessons
beneath
Saint
Mary's
Greek
Orthodox
dome.
—Home.
—Home.
—Home.
—Home.
—Home.
—Home.
—Home.

5

O
set
a
man
to
watch
all
night,
watch
all
night,
watch
all
night.
Set
a
man
to
watch
all
night,
my
fair
lady.
And
if
the
man
should
fall
asleep,
fall
asleep,
fall
asleep . . . ?

6

"Pride
of
Minneapolis,"
the
mills—
where
the
great
1878
flour-dust
explosion
leveled
neighborhoods,
killed
eighteen,
and
shook
surrounding
hills—
look
on
from
either
shore,
vacantly,
like
veterans
unable
or
unwilling
to
suffer
senseless
suffering
anymore.

7

Twenty
minutes
was
the
spell
between
my
crossing
and
when
it
fell.
Twenty
minutes
ordering
files.
Twenty
minutes
buying
meat.
Twenty
choices,
street
to
street.
To
beat
survival's
twenty
questions
"twenty
minutes"
doesn't
answer
well.

8

Innate,
isn't
it—
this
instinct
to
toss
some
speck
into
water,
to
mark
with
sprig
or
twig
that
ever
shifting
glass,
to
sprinkle
pulled
grass,
to
petal
it . . .
as
if
we
might
somehow
settle
it?

9

Disaster
reaches
in
our
direction,
and
we
reach
back
with
our
endless
questions.
Child
becomes
master;
master
child.
A
bridge
is
formed
of
these
reachings,
between
our
thirst
for
answers
and
the
world's
wild
teachings.

Each
one
as
sturdy
as
the
last,
come
scores
of
prayers
like
rescue
rings.
What
gods
did
guide
those
buoyant
things?
and
why'd
some
take
up
living
weight
and
others
come
for
some
too
late?

11

By
seven
o'clock
it's
clear
who
can
be
saved
and
who
is
gone
by
who
is
found
amid
the
half-
sunk
wrecks
and
suck-
pocked
rocks,
and
by
whose
lucks,
like
fickle
flocks,
are
flown.

12

Thunder
Woman
was
her
Indian
name.
Just
months
since
Julia
died
that
day,
the
Blackhawks
had
given
all
their
photographs
of
her
away.
Looking
back
would
only
prolong
her
journey
to
the
ancestors,
they
say.

13

These
sacred
haha
(Dakota
for
falls)—
called
mnyomni
and
mnirara—
harbored
Oanktehi,
god
of
evil,
whose
laughter
mocked
hunting
parties
who
were
forced
to
run
their
boats
aground
and
portage
around,
upon
hearing
the
sound.

14

Anything
can
happen
anytime,
you
know.
Nobody
expects
you
to
like
it,
though.
Any
minute,
the
river
of
your
life
might
drain
through
a
pinhole
burst
among
the
vessels
of
your
brain
(.)
just
so.

15

San
Francisco,
1997—
A
girl
of
two
(toddling
hand
in
hand
between
mom
and
dad)
slips
through
a
nine-
inch
gap
and
drops
to
the
glittering
Bay . . .
And
surely
they
grasp
after
her
still
today . . .

Not
water
but
air's
where
the
fallen
fall
first.
Not
landing,
but
numbing
to
the
fact
that
landing
is
coming,
is
the
worst
part
of
falling.
Not
losing
a
loved
one
but
calling
and
calling.

Among
mankind's
universal
scares:
nightmares
of
falling.
Which
of
us
hasn't
thrashed
awake,
grasping?
If
some
inspector
said
your
bed
might
buckle
and
drop
you
through
floorboards
downstairs,
how
long
would
you
hold
up
repairs?

18

Diverted
temporarily,
Minneapolis
commutes
differently,
adds
lanes
narrowly,
uses
secondary
routes
primarily,
remembers
there's
a
stream
beneath
the
grid
somewhere
down
there
(but
a
dream)
—then
goes
on
its
way
again.
Warily,
warily,
warily,
warily.

19

One
bridge
fails
and
they
all
feel
faulty.
The
Washington
and
the
Franklin
of
decline
too
are
guilty.
One
can't
help
speculating:
Which
one's
next?
And
the
map
of
the
city
proves
an
ominous
text.

20

A
worn
gusset
plate.
A
few
cruddy
bolts.
A
single
lousy
joint.
What
a
stealthy
terrorist
Time
is.
Her
work
never
through,
she
spiders
forth
her
spool
of
rust
and
with
it
re-threads
every
screw.

21

Once
we
were
Brooklyn
Bridge
sore.
Now
we
lay
rebar
and
pour.
Me,
I
have
Whitman
and
Frost.
And
you?
From
what
lone
mossed
megalith
of
stone
have
you
come
so
far
to
be
lost?

Alaskan
awhile,
I'll
forever
remember
pulling
myself
to
McCarthy
in
cabled
handcart
over
glacial
roar
from
shore
to
shore,
that
tin
trap
less
car
than
lift
chair,
the
cable
less
cable
than
schism
of
air.

23

To
break
my
heart:
park
trucks
in
one
chamber
and
tear
up
the
floor
leaving
nothing
there,
not
even
the
rebar,
then
let
the
trust
of
innocent
people
pour
through
the
other
three
of
four.

24

Poetry
rarely
commands
the
respect
afforded
the
sciences,
but
engineering
is
a
science
and
at
least
I
can
say
no
badly
aging
load–
bearing
metaphor
of
mine
ever
imploded
during
rush
hour
and
killed
anyone.

25

Earth's
third-
longest
suspension
span,
the
Tacoma
Narrows
Bridge
("Galloping
Gertie"),
its
wind-
wrangled
ribbon
finally
littering
Puget
Sound,
tested
all
mankind's
engineering
beliefs
and
now
lies
rested,
one
of
the
world's
largest
man-made
reefs.

Stand
aboard
a
ship
and
look
upward
as
it
passes
under
the
grand
Quebec
span:
The
boat
seems
moored.
You'd
swear
it
was
the
bridge,
like
some
barred
bird
overhead,
that
sped
toward,
then
fled.

27

In
private
rituals
written
by
Rudyard
Kipling,
Canadian
engineers
receive
iron
rings
rumored
forged
from
the
1907
midsection
of
the
Quebec
Bridge
which,
when
it
fell,
united
75
workmen
with
the
Saint
Lawrence
River
forever.

28

The
ring,
sized
for
the
pinkie
finger
of
your
dominant
hand,
is
designed
to
remind
you
of
your
duty
to
your
fellow
man
by
dragging
its
hammered
edge
across
every
draft
of
your
every
plan.

29

High
above
barges'
wedges,
bridges
trough
across
rivers'
edges
louder
rivers
of
drivers
while
between
one's
girders
and
the
others'
boulders
the
birds
spirit
forth
with
a
swifter
force
along
a
third
more
fluid
course.

The
new
bridge
is
glib.
Riding
its
broad
rib
feels
like
a
snub.
The
going's
too
good.
Lit
blue
at
night,
it
might
be
modern
art:
It
makes
a
point
but
it's
got
no
heart.

What
if
metaphor—
stressed
connector—
erector
of
synapse
linking
shores
together—
is
the
mother
of
collapse?
Maybe
truth
is
the
province
of
gaps.
What
if
it's
simply
our
propensity
to
order
disorder
that
inevitably
snaps?

32

Crossing,
like
reading,
suspends
us
beginning
to
end.
We
must
trust
rusting
trusses
and
rumble
over
concrete
and
abstract
constructions,
mindful
of
hidden
stresses
that
flash
past
fast,
first
to
last—
a
slip
of
fishes.

33

Catching
something
sunken,
the
black
river
flings
back
one
white
wave
riding
forever,
neither
gaining
nor
losing—
a
bird's
lost
breast
feathers,
a
wrinkled
white
kerchief—
the
black
stream
seeming
blacker
against
the
shoreline
birches.

34

Some
say
that
to
the
gods
we
are
like
the
flies
boys
kill
on
a
summer's
day.
Some
say
the
very
sparrows
do
not
lose
a
feather
that
the
finger
of
God
didn't
brush
away.

35

By
singing
of
beginnings
the
great
folk
hymn
ends:
*When
we've
been
here
ten
thousand
years
bright
shining
as
the
sun,
we've
no
less
days
to
sing
God's
praise
than
when
we've
first
begun.*
Amen.

A Blessing

May the good
Lord grant you
a little pride,

since of Creation
He Himself was
more than a little

satisfied. And
while He's at it
may He cede

some greed,
from Heaven
where His gold is

guaranteed.
And envy too
upon ye pour,

He who will not
suffer any other
gods before.

And wrath!—oh,
yes, God grant
you wrath;

Noah knows
how much
God hath.

A glutton for
praise, may He
see and raise ye

(if He can admit
He's got 'ny)
gluttony.

And I protest:
if all men must
steer clear of lust,

how come He
carved Eve such
a curvy bust?

It isn't just.
Seven flames
for the moth;

the Arsonist on
His arse, too lazy
to snuff them out,

the sloth.

Visitation on the Eve of Thanksgiving

This morning three angels
a man and two women
descended from Heaven and
strode into my kitchen
in order to behold me peeling
an enormous round and
thick-rinded orange. I mean
the rind was so thick it was
like pulling a softball apart
to the cork. No that's not
right. It was more like lifting
a white mink coat from the
sun-goldened shoulders
of a beautiful woman. For
your sake reader and for
the sake of those angels I
really want to get this right
the sponge of that peel in
my hands falling apart where
my thumbnails broke its
pithy terrycloth weather and
tore those clouds away to
reveal the sunrise underneath.

I was thinking about belief.
I hadn't had my coffee yet.
And I want to get back to
those angels but first I must
tell you about last night
which is what I was thinking
about when those angels
strode into my life. Last night
my wife and I sat at the table
reading (and I know this

sounds corny but) reading
the Bible (two Bibles actually
hers an Amplified and mine
the King James). I suppose
we'd had too much good red
wine or something and got
to talking about the origin of
some proverb or another. We
took turns reading passages
to each other. We had a few
good laughs at the really
dumb parables and alternately
fell respectfully quiet
after a psalm or a song of
Solomon sounded as sound
as a sonnet. It's been years
since I opened mine. I boasted
I could still recite the books
of the Bible in order but I
tried and found they'd come
apart in my mind like un-
linked strings of paper rings
but I still had a few good
runs and ended with the
witchy ones Zephaniah Haggai
Zechariah Malachi and I'd
like to get one more thing
right about that night before
I revisit the angels because
that Bible pliant in my hands
again brought back to mind
my love of thick softcover
books which I think was the
greatest gift my Bible ever

gave me and the smell of it
and the feel of those tissue
pages flying by beneath my
thumbs it was like water or
like sand or like the fine
blonde hair of little girls
riding down a playground
slide. In confirmation class

I sat in the back row next
to a butch girl who chewed
snoose through every lesson
and spat the juice into an
empty A&W root beer can
and liked to reach across
the table and with her ball-
point pen print upon the
pages of my Bible in red or
blue the well-practiced logos
of the bands she listened to
Black Sabbath AC/DC
Mötley Crüe. She wore black
jeans and brown leather.
She had a bad older brother
and smelled like danger we
all steered clear of her and I
swear she was God's gift to
First Lutheran Church.

Anyway these angels this
morning as I was saying
strode in very matter of fact
and said We just came to
watch you peel that orange

and lo I understood then
the sadness of angels
because peeling an orange
like unraveling a story is
among earthly pleasures
one of the sweetest and
one of the advantages of
being an angel is that you
can leave the straits of
Heaven whenever you want
and for whatever reason.

Did you read in *The New
York Times* about the girl
who can feel no pain and
therefore lives in fear of
her body in the physical
world? As a toddler, she
took the muffler of her
father's powerwasher in
both hands and didn't flinch
while the flesh was cooking.
O Lord of Life, spare us
from the painless place
you've promised. And
on this plane grant us
enough ugliness and grief
to throw beauty and joy
into relief. As for you,

O Reader, I wish you
could've seen them
watch me pull it open
the orange in all their eyes

flowering and dropping its
heavy clothing. It must
be hard to die and be denied
this luscious world for all
eternity and to have to hold
fast to the belief that it
once existed and still
does. How can you blame
them? How can you blame
them for wanting proof,
after all their years aloft,
adrift, aloof in the soft
cotton linen rooms of
Heaven, proof that men
still stand in their robes
in kitchens, dismantling
muscular globes of oranges
in the far-flung corridors
of the morning sun? An
eternity in the extraordinary
must feed a certain greed
for the mundane, the one
thing God, in all his glory,
can't give us again.

Eve

How could she—twisting it from her teeth
for the first time, sugarsap rivering like meath
down wrist and chin, her tastelets shivering
from that first crunch-spritz & its delivering
pomblast & peel-sting, its pithmash a perfect
discrumpulation in the mouth, so fruct-
uously crushbursting & rush-luscious—yes,

how could she *not*, on finishing the best
crash course in astonishment naturally devised—
how could she not have looked into his eyes
as juices further traced her waist, her breast,
& beckoned him to sample from the rest—
& how could he, her husbander, her flesh,
not take & eat & champ the world afresh—?

When You Teach the East or West Coast Swing

you can't

not men-
tion ten-

sion, for
never

was a pass
or a

push off a
rock–

step
strong–

er than when
steady as a

rock was
that which

off against it
went, nor

never was a
girl sent spin–

bent surer
to return

and be caught
and be caught

without a
hitch than

by one taught
that one taut

finger
on the switch

can be the
scratch

that strikes
the match

that lights
the fuse

that makes
the evening

bloom
—boom!—

and keeps
the room

beneath
her shoes.

Soon I Wake Among New Hills

                    : new hips,
new thighs, new
breasts banked
in blankets as if
in mists, my
chest and flanks the
flat fields beneath,

a new New Hampshire,
a new Vermont.

I wake a landscape
myself and in myself.

I'd swear there are
tiny flocks crossing,
motes in windowlight,

tiny flocks crossing
in raking patterns,
raking the sky clear
of the past.

And soon enough: and
fast: I fall asleep in
that sweet homeland,

tiny flocks crossing
  tiny flocks crossing
tiny flocks crossing

from the faraway
footlands to the
soft white mountains
at the head of the bed.

How Naturally

—having
shown her

that a little
white sugar

brings out
the berry's

deeper nectar
by dropping

between her
teeth one

pluperfect
exemplar—

I linger
to offer

the driblets
of juice

on my finger
for her

to kiss after.

I'd Like to Go Through All Your Rooms

one by one and turn out lights

and unplug appliances so there's
nothing left humming or

glowing or ticking or storing
anything in memory or listening

for the radio beam of a remote
to tell it what it ought to do

and then I'd like to lay you down
in a quiet as deep as blankets

and let the snow do all the hard
thinking that still needs doing and

put the moon in charge of making
old ideas new again and then

I'd like to put my hands against
whatever you've got in storage

and push it across your attic floor
so there's room for us to do

what we don't need one damned
thing in the world to do while

out on the lawn the auctioneer
begins the bidding oh yes the

bidding who will start the bidding
and let the bidding of the cosmos

yes yes the bidding of the cosmos
going once going twice undo us

of everything worldly we possess.

Grinding Coffee

I turn its hand-turned rock maple turn-handle in my hand
and the morning's first bargain's begun—a rather grand
handshake that winds the S-crank that cranks in turn twinned
chamfered burrs internally, through which, from a jar upturned
above, the beans that will become my coffee tumble and grind
to land in an inconstant crumble in a catch-cup below. Round
and round and round—a monkey's organ with a single sound,
turning the wall it's mounted on into a kind of soundboard and
my kitchen to a bandstand, the tune a tuneless free-jazz brand
of washboard waltz. Talk halts till the hurdy-gurdy's ground
to an end. All that's left is beanmillery, an ounce of jet-black
sand. The teapot murmurs, then grumbles about eternity—and
I pour.
    To employ an antique thing is to keep an old friend.

And now the room's all aroma. And the quiet's returned.

AMMO and EXPLOSIVES

shout the antique
wooden boxes in
antique letters all

over my quarters
—album hoarders,
planters, magazine
holders, markers

of borders—&
why do I love them,
love their dove-
tailed corners,

their softened
block typographies
stenciled above
gross weights

& quantities,
their sturdy
eloquence after
so many years?

oh, it's usefulness
I admire I guess,
though they're
shells of their

former selves
like old dogs
on whose deaf
ears praise falls

but who still
find ways to get
their one trick
done with

diligence, or like
retirees who still
fix things, vets
who still pray

over dinner
no matter the
bread & who–
ever the winner.

When My Glasses Went Lost in Clearwater

the $5 reward I offered that night at dinner
lit lights in the eyes of the younger campers
bright enough that in the morning hours
one named August brought an august air
into the room where I was teaching there,
and, dripping wet from his expedition,
and trailing behind him a boys' delegation,
calmly approached my podium,
reverently presented them,
posed to greet the elder group's applause,
claimed his prize, then led the boys outdoors
to run the grounds again from lake to lea,
and see the world for all we could not see.

I Find It Lovely That We Name Our Boats

and that
somewhere

someone you wouldn't suspect of gentleness

kisses
the reed–

gold
bristles

of a brush
into the

blood–
red paint

in the tin can cupped in his hand and softly slips its

silken
gloss

off
into the

curve of a
cursive

S or *W* or
N and

thereby begins the name at stern that steers a formerly

unnamed
skiff or

sloop into
the calmer

waters of
the claimed

and tethers it there—knot by loop knot—

like a pet
or a mapped

spot or a
fish caught

in a rope net.

A Hoard of Driftwood

From a sandy stretch of Superior shore one summer
I hoarded a store of tidbits plundered from the driftline:
a glassine shard of hardwood lake-rinsed almost down
to carbon, a flaxen ribbon of rootstem flute-furled,
an oaken knuckle uncoupled from the knot that once
whorled it, a gnarl from a thicker uncoupling laved
smooth as a buckle from ruckling wave upon wave,
a nickel of cambium written with rays as if rift-sawn,
a rickrack of spoondrift pine turned ebon, a pillowy
chip of pulleywheel or some likewise ligneous tackle,
and a bindle of sticks spun spindle-thin, silken as scallion.
All dry-weight, drier than stone but thin as air, finer than
hair and softer than skin—as if despite the unintended sin
of being broken down, they'd been born again, beauty-strong.

Petoskey Stone

A hundred thousand years old, you said,
but I looked it up:
Four hundred million's more like it, Dad.

Still, what's a couple thousand
centamillennia more or less?—Man
might as well have stood erect
just yesterday
for all he's come to. Doesn't matter.
You wanted to make a gift and you were trying
to say it was special. That's why
as our summer vacation wore on,
you sanded every day
the Petoskey stone you'd found onshore,
sanded it smooth and smoother
with a fine black wet sandpaper,
to illuminate the coral core
fossilized in there, and I was reminded
how I hated standing
at your workbench as a boy, sanding
some work of hardwood, practicing patience
abominably. After the rough stuff,
the numbers get higher
and the sawdust finer and the pores
in the grain take on a radiant sheen you'd
never dreamed was there. The pores
in one's fingers absorb more and more
of the finer dusts, so that soon it seems
one's made of wood oneself,
as indeed we are, as wood is made of us.

I hated that tedium, hated it,
and yet here I am now, smoothing it down,
this poem, revising and revising it,

doubtful it will ever be done—
wanting to make something lasting
of the offhand way he gave that stone,
polished to a sheen, to my son.

Wild Again

In the end, they let it
go wild again, un-
made the mile of
fence they'd made,
rolled fencewire onto
rolls and sold them,
sold the fencepost,
sold the hardware,
sold the wire puller,
wire-cutter, post-
hole digger, filled
the holes so they'd
harm neither deer nor
hunter. Oh let them go

wild again, they said
of the fields they'd
tended twenty years,
the aspens and firs
the first to trespass,
seeds and cones un-
furling into seedlings
in ryegrass/timothy/
brome. The seasons
browned, snowed,
greened and so on,
and soon their rise

was wild again with
birches and brush,
good cover for foxes,
for thrush, a flush of
pheasant, a pleasant
blush of shade where

once only sunshine
was wanted, the black–
berry's barbs tangling
forth now, and to the
north now storm–
bent walnuts angling
walnuts down upon
an unmown lawn gone

wild again. Wild again
the lane and wild the
logging road, the ruts
each spring with a fuller–
throated frogmass filling,
the cottonwood spilling
its lissome sex into
the clover, the farmers'
labors over. Long they
argued with the earth
and the earth has won.
Now it's not a man's but
a god's farm, a garden,
the fallen Eden, earthen
heaven, kingdom of
the tree, and the farmer
free.

In the End a Gardener

is what we want in our corner
of paradise. Someone alert
to the slant of one hour
of afternoon sunlight or other,
who knows what to plant there,
knows what will thrive.
We strive after someone
content to strive—patient
as *impatiens* and tenacious
as *tanacetum*. As we get older,
men trend a lot more flora
than fauna, drawn not
to hunter, owner or tamer,
but to friend—to one whose
tendency is simply *to tend*.
Whose prayer is her answer.
In the end, despite what we
formerly went for, a gardener
is the godsend we bend for.

for Kitty and Jack

A Bouquet

Autumns ago, from a woodland path I take,
I took enough weather-wizened weeds to make
a vaseful: one cattail, four wands of tallgrass
limping furred lists of seed and trailing a mass
of ribboncurled leavings, three eyes of Susan
healed of blackness but all unpetaled, one
seedpod-mottled cob-column that once flaunted
stalk-bloom, a claque of twist-cones that sounded
a rattle when I picked them, grayed golden-
rods goitered with the balls of gall flies long gone
larva-less, two marvelous razzles of tiny white
tuft-cups, and a clutch of leathered fuzzes, tight
from thirst. Paupers all—sexless and blind—
still calling summer's dazzles to my mind.

One of the Joys of Dry Fly-Fishing

is the chance of matching with grace
the grace of the place one fishes in.

Where other men make plunk and
spin, we silent dry fly fishermen
make signatures of gossamer in air.

Where other men write prose, we cast
poetic lines about, so as not to catch
so much as rhyme ourselves with trout.

for Johnny

Acknowledgments

The author gratefully acknowledges the periodicals in which these poems first appeared:

Alaska Quarterly Review: "For an Old Runner"

Alhambra Poetry Calendar: "Blessing"

Dunes Review: "A Bouquet"
"In the End a Gardener"
"How Naturally"
"One of the Joys of Dry Fly-Fishing"

Georgia Review: "AMMO and EXPLOSIVES"

Poetry: "Accounting"
"Bravery"
"Rocket"

PRISM International: "Folds"
"A Hoard of Driftwood"
"I Find It Lovely That We Name
Our Boats"
"Petoskey Stone"

Star Tribune: "Fragments for the 35W Bridge"

Terrain: "When My Father Says *Toughen Up*"
"When My Mother Says *Tough Luck*"
"When We Say *Knuckle Down*"

Additional acknowledgments: "When We Say *Knuckle Down*" was anthologized in *Best of the Net 2015*. "The Mind Will Wander" was anthologized in *What Light*, a publication of MNartists.org. "Fragments for the 35W Bridge" was available by phone in mixed voices produced by Maja Spasova as part of "Project 35W," a collaborative installation on the Mississippi River in 2012 consisting of thirty-five oversized life rings anchored in the water. Five of the "Fragments" are reprinted from *Pitch* (W. W. Norton, 2012). "Rocket" and "Bravery" were reprinted in *Poetry Daily*.

NOTES on the poems

Fragments for the 35W Bridge:

"Catching something sunken . . ." (Fragment 33) quotes from a stanza of Robert Frost's "West-Running Brook."

"The river enters the gulf…" (Fragment 1) draws upon lines by Lucille Clifton from her poem "the mississippi river empties into the gulf," which is reprinted here in full.

the mississippi river empties into the gulf

and the gulf enters the sea and so forth,
none of them emptying anything,
all of them carrying yesterday
forever on their white tipped backs,
all of them dragging forward tomorrow.
it is the great circulation
of the earth's body, like the blood
of the gods, this river in which the past
is always flowing. every water
is the same water coming round.
everyday someone is standing on the edge
of this river, staring into time,
whispering mistakenly:
only here. only now.

Lucille Clifton, "the mississippi empties into the gulf," from *Collected Poems of Lucille Clifton.* Copyright © 1996 by Lucille Clifton. Reprinted with the permission of The Permissions Company, Inc., on behalf of BOA Editions, Ltd., www.boaeditions.org.

"O set a man to watch all night" (Fragment 5) is a verse from the traditional song "London Bridge Is Falling Down."

"Some say . . . brush away" (Fragment 34) paraphrases the last paragraph of Chapter 1 of Thornton Wilder's novel *The Bridge of San Luis Rey.*

"*When we've been here ten thousand years . . .*" (Fragment 35) is the last verse of John Newton's "Amazing Grace."

THANKS

The *Star Tribune* has maintained an excellent multimedia website devoted to telling the stories of the people who were on the 35W Bridge when it collapsed.

Marine historian Dan Conlin mentioned Canada's Iron Ring ritual to me on Garrison Keillor's "A Prairie Home Companion" cruise, which passed beneath the Quebec Bridge in 2011.

Thanks to readers Kirsten Dierking, Tim Nolan, Sharon Chmielarz, Liz Weir, Dore Kiesselbach, John Hermanson, Jack Miles, and Jaime Davis.